Ten magic tricks with French

By Lucy Martin

TABLE OF CONTENTS

With thanks to Phil and Victoria for proof reading as learners, and to every dyslexic child I have taught for inspiring me to come up with the magic tricks. Thank you for letting me into your world. Thank you also to all the enthusiastic students who never get genders wrong anymore, proving that this book really does what it says on the front cover.

My dear apprentices

French is not such a difficult language if you use a few basic rules and memory techniques. Using a combination of audio and visual "imagination journeys", a student can bypass some of the technical stuff and master aspects of the language that may have remained a mystery since the beginning. To others it will seem like magic, but for you it's just a case of learning a few tricks.

The first common area of confusion is around the articles and prepositions we use with nouns. In English, we say *"dogs are nice"*, *"I play tennis"*, *"we play cards"*, *"I prefer swimming"* or *"I would like more pudding"* without using any sort of article, but in French you can't leave those words "chiens", "tennis", "cartes", "natation", and "dessert" sitting alone. They need a little word in front, but how do you choose from this little selection: *un / une / le / la / du / des / au / à la / aux*? This is all dealt with in Tricks 1-4.

The second area of difficulty for many students is verbs. Very few of us have the patience or the inclination to memorise endless verb endings. By using my rhymes and pictures as a reference point, and retaining *those*, instead of the verbs themselves, you will make much more sense of this minefield and become proficient at identifying the tenses and employing them in speech and writing. Tricks 5-8 deal with all your basic verbs and the main three tenses – present, past and future. (I do not cover the imperfect, the near future or the conditional in this book.)

The third area is using prepositions with places and transport, saying where you're going and how you're getting there. When do you use *en, à, au, à la, aux, à l'*? Trick 9 will show you. The last trick is all about the weather. And you know how much we like to talk about that.

When you have mastered every trick in the book, (literally), you will have a very good handle on the basics of French and will be ready to move on to my next book, *Advancing your French*.

I use the term *"magic tricks"* with a certain irony, but having seen the way students respond and the speed at which their grades rocket, I make no apology, and I'm confident that any student of GCSE or Common entrance, as well as students in other parts of the world studying French, will find themselves enormously better equipped to deal with the demands of French in the classroom once they have been through this short workbook.

The answers are on the page after each exercise, so self-discipline (or a supervising adult) may be required in order to reap the full benefit. I suggest that to make the most of the book you write the answers on a separate sheet rather than in here, and redo the exercises until you get 100% every time. The essential vocabulary lists at the back also provide a few tips on getting words into your memory, and contain some of the key words that appear repeatedly in exams.

One final note is that this book is not exhaustive. There will be exceptions to all the rules if you look hard enough. But I would advise anyone taking Common Entrance or GCSE French to stick to what you know – don't go trying out new expressions and vocab in the exam that you don't know for sure is correct. Don't mention countries, food and activities you have never tried mentioning before.

Have fun learning! (Because that's what learning should always be)

Lucy   Your personal magician

SOME BASICS BEFORE YOU START

Un or *Une* both mean *"a"* depending on whether the noun is masculine or feminine

un garçon	a boy
une fille	a girl
un chien	a dog
une pomme	an apple

Mon / ma / mes all mean *"my"* depending on whether the noun (the person / thing that belongs to you) is masculine, feminine or plural

mon frère	my brother
ma mère	my mother
mes parents	my parents

Same applies for ton / ta / tes (your) and son / sa / ses (his or her)

Le / la / les all mean *"the"*, depending on whether the noun is masculine, feminine or plural

le chien	the dog
la maison	the house
les enfants	the children

But there are times when you use le / la / les when there is no *the* in English at all. The first is with school subjects:

J'étudie l'histoire et la géo	I am studying history and geography
J'étudie les maths et le latin	I study maths and Latin

AND the second is on the next page…

TRICK 1

Liking (and preferring / <u>disliking</u>) things is followed by L

This means the next word in the sentence will be *le, la* or *les*. When we express our like or dislike of something, it is for the thing in general, and le la les refers to the thing in general rather than a specific one, or a specific group. I like dogs / sports / chips means I like them in general.

j'aime les chiens	I like dogs
Il préfère les chats	He prefers cats
Elle adore la neige	She loves snow
J'aime beaucoup le chocolat	I like chocolate very much
Je déteste la viande	I hate meat
Je n'aime pas les documentaires	I don't like documentaries

(But liking activities is followed by the infinitive)

J'aime mang**er**	I like to eat
Il déteste nag**er**	He hates swimming
J'aime beaucoup dessin**er**	I like drawing a lot
Elle préfère dorm**ir**	She prefers sleeping
Je n'aime pas cour**ir**	I don't like running
J'adore regard**er** la télévision	I love watching TV (*the* TV in French)

Opinions and justifications are important in your writing and speaking

Je n'aime pas les films romantiques parce qu'ils sont ennuyeux.   Je préfère les films d'action parce que les effets spéciaux sont incroyables.

I don't like romantic films because they are boring. I prefer action films because the special effects are incredible.

J'adore nager parce que c'est relaxant et je suis sportif

I love swimming because it's relaxing and I am sporty

Before you do the test on the page opposite, take a moment to think about what you have learnt in this first lesson....

Testing you on Trick 1

1. I like chocolate

2. I like dogs

3. I like snow

4. I like eating

5. I like playing

6. I like watching the TV

7. I don't like watching the TV

8. I hate dogs

9. I don't like chocolate

10. I love listening to music

11. I hate meat

12. I prefer sweets

13. I hate playing football

14. I prefer playing rugby

15. I prefer rugby

Answers

1.	I like dogs	J'aime les chiens
2.	I like chocolate	J'aime le chocolat
3.	I like snow	J'aime la neige
4.	I like eating	J'aime manger
5.	I like playing	J'aime jouer
6.	I like watching the TV	J'aime regarder la télé
7.	I don't like watching the TV	Je n'aime pas regarder la télé
8.	I hate dogs	Je déteste les chiens
9.	I don't like chocolate	Je n'aime pas le chocolat
10.	I love listening to music	J'adore écouter de la musique
11.	I hate meat	Je déteste la viande
12.	I prefer sweets	Je préfère les bonbons
13.	I hate playing football	Je déteste jouer au foot
14.	I prefer playing rugby	Je préfère jouer au rugby
15.	I prefer rugby	Je préfère le rugby

TRICK 2   Pas de, beaucoup de – specific amounts

"De" basically means "of". So, if there is a lot of (beaucoup de), too much of (trop de), too many of (trop de), more of (plus de), less of (moins de) something, then it's not a big surprise that you're going to use **de**. But whereas we might say "there is more pollution" that's where the French will be different "*il y a plus de pollution*".) All of these are expressions of quantity.

Beaucoup / trop / plus / moins / assez + de

Il y a beaucoup de bruit	There is a lot of noise
Il y a trop de chiens	There are too many dogs
Il y a plus d'enfants	There are more children
Il y a moins de pollution	There is less pollution
Il y a assez de place	There is enough room
J'ai beaucoup d'argent	I have a lot of money
J'ai beaucoup de copains	I have lots of friends

Another time you will use "de" is after a negated verb, ie a verb in the negative, such as *I don't eat, I don't do, I don't have.* This does not apply to *all* verbs, but just remember it for having, eating and doing for now.

Ne ….pas + de

Je n'ai pas d'argent	I don't have any money
Il n'y a pas de pistes cyclables	There aren't any cycle paths
Il ne mange pas de viande	He doesn't eat meat
Je ne fais pas de sport	I don't do sport

Don't forget that **Trick one, the rule about liking, takes precedence** over this one, so only move on to this if you have ruled out the first rule, as it were. AND j'aime beaucoup is a type of liking so takes *le / la / les*!

Using tricks 1 and 2 in practice

1. What do you have a lot of?
2. What do you have none of?
3. What is there a lot of / too much of in your town?
4. In the countryside what is there less of?
5. Do you prefer town or countryside?
6. Do you like school? Why?
7. What isn't there at your school?

Example :

J'ai beaucoup de lapins mais je n'ai pas de chien. J'ai beaucoup de jeux-video mais je n'ai pas de Playstation. Dans ma ville il y a beaucoup de voitures et trop de pollution, et il y a beaucoup de bruit. A la campagne il y a moins de circulation que dans la ville. J'aime la campagne parce que c'est tranquille mais je préfère la ville parce qu'il y a plus de distractions. J'aime mon collège parce que c'est animé et moderne mais il n'y a pas de piscine.

I have lots of rabbits but I don't have a dog. I have lots of video games but I don't have a Playstation. In my town there are lots of cars and too much pollution and there is a lot of noise. In the countryside there is less traffic than in the town. I like the countryside because it's quieter but I prefer the town because there are more things to do. I like my school because it's lively and modern but there isn't a swimming pool.

Now answer questions 1-7 above in a paragraph *of your own* to practice this:

……………………………………………………………………………………………..

……………………………………………………………………………………………..

……………………………………………………………………………………………..

……………………………………………………………………………………………..

……………………………………………………………………………………………..

……………………………………………………………………………………………..

Testing you on Tricks 1 and 2

1. I like French

2. I don't like dogs

3. I prefer apples

4. I hate pollution

5. I love weekends

6. I don't have a cat

7. There isn't any noise

8. I don't eat meat

9. I don't do sport

10. I don't like carrots

11. I don't have any carrots

12. I don't like horror films

13. There isn't a cinema

14. There are too many cars

15. There are fewer cars

16. There are more green spaces

17. I like eating

18. I don't like doing my homework

19. I like lots of sports

20. I like maths a lot

Answers

1. I like French   J'aime le français

2. I don't like dogs   Je n'aime pas les chiens

3. I prefer apples   Je préfère les pommes

4. I hate pollution   Je déteste la pollution

5. I love weekends   J'adore les week-ends

6. I don't have a cat   Je n'ai pas de chat

7. There isn't any noise   Il n'y a pas de bruit

8. I don't eat meat   Je ne mange pas de viande

9. I don't do sport   Je ne fais pas de sport

10. I don't like carrots   Je n'aime pas les carottes

11. I don't have any carrots   Je n'ai pas de carottes

12. I don't like horror films   Je n'aime pas les films d'horreur

13. There isn't a cinema   Il n'y a pas de cinéma

14. There are too many cars   Il y a trop de voitures

15. There are fewer cars   Il y a moins de voitures

16. There are more green spaces   Il y a plus d'espaces verts

17. I like eating   J'aime manger

18. I don't like doing my homework   Je n'aime pas faire mes devoirs

19. I like lots of sports   J'aime beaucoup de sports

20. I like maths a lot   J'aime beaucoup les maths (type of liking!)

TRICK 3   Activities

Sometimes an activity verb is going to be a literal translation of the English:

lire – je lis le journal   I read the paper

regarder – je regarde la télé   I watch the TV

écouter – j'écoute le prof   I listen to the teacher

But with activities relating to exercise, music and technology, you will need to use **jouer** or **faire**. You need to ask yourself:

1. Is it a **game** that you play and can win?   If so, say **je joue au**
    (use "aux" for chess – *échecs* - and cards -*cartes* - as they are plural

    Je joue au tennis   I play tennis

    Je joue au netball   I play netball

    Je joue au basket   I play basketball

    Je joue aux cartes / aux échecs   I play cards / chess

2. Is it an **instrument**? If so it's **je joue du / de la**

    Je joue du piano   (*du du du* goes the piano)

    Je joue de la guitare   (*la la la* singing to the guitar)

3. Is it **technology**? If so you can use **je joue sur**

    Je joue sur mon ordinateur/portable   I play on my computer / phone

    Je joue sur ma PlayStation   I play on my PlayStation

Je joue sur ma Xbox   I play on my XBox

REMINDER jouer is not a verb covered by Trick 2, so just use ne … pas as you would expect to here eg je ne joue pas sur mon ordinateur / au tennis.

If it isn't covered by jouer, you must go to *faire* land *(Fairyland).*

There are **no balls allowed in fairyland**, (all ball games use jouer) and no music or technology, but it's full of activities. You won't be bored…

In fairyland, you can use **"Je fais du"** – with most activities

- **Je fais du** sport   I do sport *(no playing sport)*
- **Je fais du** vélo, du cyclisme   I cycle
- **Je fais du** VTT   I go mountain biking
- **Je fais du** patinage   I go skating
- **Je fais du** judo   I do judo
- **Je fais du** karaté   I do karate
- **Je fais du** ski (nautique)   I ski / I go waterskiing
- **Je fais du** footing, du jogging   I go jogging

But with the feminine activities, use **"je fais de la"**

Imagine you are swimming in the sea, and to the left of you there is someone windsurfing, on the right there is someone sailing, and on the sea bed there is some scuba diving going on. Looking back at the beach, you see people dancing, doing gym and weights on the sand. Every activity in that scene uses *je fais de la*. The scene is to help you remember the feminine activities. Sometimes we say "go" in English when we mean "do" so watch out!

Je fais de la

- **Je fais de la** natation   I go swimming
- **Je fais de la** voile   I sail
- **Je fais de la** planche à voile   I go windsurfing
- **Je fais de la** plongée   I scuba dive
- **Je fais de la** gymnastique   I do gymnastics
- **Je fais de la** danse   I dance
- **Je fais de la** musculation   I do weight training

If the activity begins with a vowel use **"je fais de l'"**

- **Je fais de l'**équitation   I go horseriding
- **Je fais de l'**alpinisme   I go mountaineering
- **Je fais de l'**athlétisme   I do athletics
- **Je fais de l'**escalade   I go climbing
- **Je fais de l'**escrime   I do fencing

if you do lots of them, like walks, use **je fais des**

Je fais des randonnées / promenades   I go hiking / walking

16

Put the activities in the right column

Foot, cricket, échecs, piano, guitare, ordinateur, Xbox, rugby, hockey, netball, basket, cartes, volley, PS4, tennis, portable

Je joue au	Je joue aux	Je joue sur mon	Je joue sur ma	Je joue du (du du du)	Je joue de la (la la la)

Natation, voile, cyclisme, VTT, équitation, promenades, vélo, gymnastique, danse, plongée, planche à voile, ski-nautique, alpinisme, escrime, escalade, athlétisme, judo, karaté, sport, patinage, randonnées, footing, ski, jogging

Je fais du	Je fais de la (beach)	Je fais de l' (vowel)	Je fais des (plural)

Answers

Je joue au	Je joue aux	Je joue sur mon	Je joue sur ma	Je joue du	Je joue de la
foot cricket rugby hockey netball basket volley	échecs cartes	ordinateur portable	Xbox PS4	piano	guitare

Je fais du	Je fais de la	Je fais de l'	Je fais des
VTT vélo judo karaté sport patinage ski ski-nautique cyclisme	natation voile planche à voile gymnastique danse plongée	équitation alpinisme escrime escalade athlétisme	promenades randonnées

Reminder of the order of tricks:

1. if it's liking, disliking, preferring, it's **le la les**
   So, to say you like sport it's *j'aime le sport.*
2. if you don't have it, or do it, or if you **have** or **do** a lot of it, it's **de**
   To say you don't do it, *je ne fais pas de sport.*
3. Then (as long as it's not taken by "jouer") you can go to fairyland
. To say you do it, it's *je fais du sport.*

Examples

I like football (caught by trick 1)	j'aime le foot
I play football (tricks 1 and 2 don't apply so go to 3)	je joue au foot
I don't like football (caught by trick 1)	je n'aime pas le foot
I do a lot of sport **(no liking, but caught by 2)**	je fais beaucoup de sport
I like playing rugby (caught by trick 1 with verb)	j'aime jouer au rugby
I so a lot of swimming **(caught by 2)**	je fais beaucoup de natation
I don't do any swimming **(caught by trick 2)**	je ne fais pas de natation
I like swimming a lot (caught by trick 1)	j'aime beaucoup la natation
I like lots of sports **(caught by trick 2)**	j'aime beaucoup de sports
I do sport (tricks 1 and 2 don't apply so go to 3)	je fais du sport

Now you're on your own...

1. I do a lot of judo

2. I go skating a lot

3. I don't go (do) swimming

4. I like swimming

5. I like going (doing) swimming

6. I like playing football

7. I don't do sport

8. I go (do) swimming

9. I like sport a lot

10. I like lots of sports

Answers

1. I do a lot of judo   je fais beaucoup de judo
   (caught by trick 2)

2. I go (do) skating a lot   je fais beaucoup de patinage
   (caught by trick 2)

3. I don't go (do) swimming   je ne fais pas de natation
   (caught by trick 2)

4. I like swimming   J'aime la natation OR j'aime nager
   (caught by trick 1)

5. I like going (doing) swimming   J'aime faire de la natation
   (caught by trick 1 – liking with verbs takes infinitive)

6. I like playing football   J'aime jouer au foot
   (caught by trick 1 – liking with verbs takes infinitive)

7. I don't do sport   Je ne fais pas de sport
   (caught by trick 2)

8. I go (do) swimming   Je fais de la natation
   (not caught by trick 1 or 2 so you can go to fairyland!)

9. I like sport a lot   J'aime beaucoup le sport
   (caught by trick 1 because J'aime beaucoup is a type of liking)

10. I like lots of sports   J'aime beaucoup de sports
    (trick 2 because the liking stops after j'aime, and beaucoup is in control of what follows)

Before you go on, take a moment to tell yourself, as if you were another person new to this, what Tricks 1-4 are all about.

RICK 4   Food

If doesn't fit into tricks 1-3, then the door opens wide and you can use *un / une / du / de la* or *des*. The main area you will use this for is food, (*I ate chicken and chips / do you have bread?*) but it works for most other things too, like money, tickets, stamps. In English we can either:

* miss out the article entirely ("they have cats")
* use the word "some" ("I ate some bread", "I bought some chocolate / stamps", "I've got some jam / money")
* use the word "any" ("do you have any bread / chocolate / stamps / money?")

But In French, you can't leave a noun on its own, and there isn't a standard word for "*some*" or "*any*". Normallly we are talking about eating and drinking, especially at GCSE, so let's stick to that for now, and here is the rhyme

"The food I ate today is un, une, du, de la or des"

1) Do you eat the whole thing?   .... **un / une**

J'ai mangé **une pomme**   *I ate an apple*
Il mange **un hamburger**   *He eats a burger*

2) Is it plural? Do you eat lots of them?   .... **des**

J'ai mangé **des frites**   *I ate chips*
Il mange **des champignons**   *He eats mushrooms*

3) Is it on my red list? - pizza, jam, meat, sauce, soup, ice cream
(*pretend it is strawberry*). *This is not* just *any* red food   .... **de la**

J'ai mangé **de la pizza, de la viande, de la soupe, de la sauce,** et puis **de la glace** avec **de la confiture** *I ate pizza, meat, soup, sauce and then ice cream with jam*

4) None of the above? .... **du**
(mostly picnic food – bread, butter, cheese, ham, chicken)

J'ai mangé **du pain** avec **du fromage** et **du jambon** *I ate bread with cheese and ham*

Remember you still need to keep the first two tricks in mind even with food, because if you like it, or have a lot of it, or none of them, it will follow Trick 1 or Trick 2. Look at these examples:

Trick 1 examples are about chocolate in general ("choc" for short)

J'aime le chocolat (I like choc)	caught by trick 1
Je n'aime pas le chocolat (I don't like choc)	caught by trick 1
Je préfère le chocolat (I prefer choc)	caught by trick 1
Je déteste le chocolat (I hate choc)	caught by trick 1
J'aime beaucoup le chocolat (I like choc a lot)	caught by trick 1

Trick 2 examples are about specific amounts of chocolate

J'ai beaucoup de chocolat (I have lots of choc)	caught by trick 2
J'aime beaucoup de chocolat (I like lots of choc)	caught by trick 2
Je n'ai pas de chocolat (I don't have any choc)	caught by trick 2
Il n'y a pas de chocolat (There isn't any choc)	caught by trick 2
Il y a trop de chocolat (There is too much choc)	caught by trick 2
Il y a plus de chocolat (There is more choc)	caught by trick 2
Il y a moins de chocolat (There is less choc)	caught by trick 2

Trick 4 is about some or any chocolate

Je voudrais du chocolat	not 1 or 2 or fairyland so TRICK 4
Vous avez du chocolat?	not 1 or 2 or fairyland so TRICK 4
Je mange du chocolat	not 1 or 2 or fairyland so TRICK 4
J'ai mangé du chocolat	not 1 or 2 or fairyland so TRICK 4

Food vocab – cover up the right hand side and see how many you know

du pain	bread
du beurre	butter
du fromage	cheese
du poulet	chicken
du jambon	ham
du saucisson	sausage
du poisson	fish
du gâteau	cake
du chocolat	chocolate
du lait	milk
du vin	wine
de la viande	meat
de la confiture	jam
de la glace	ice cream
de la pizza	pizza
de la soupe	soup
de la sauce	sauce
de l'agneau	lamb
de l'eau	water
des chips	crisps *(not chips!)*
des frites	chips *(fries!)*
des céréales	cereal *(remember it's plural)*
des pâtes	pasta *(remember it's plural)*
des œufs	eggs
des légumes	vegetables
des pommes de terre	potatoes
des petits pois	peas
des haricots verts	green beans
des champignons	mushrooms
des oignons	onions
une pomme	an apple
un ananas	a pineapple

Using the rules on page 22, put these in the correct columns to describe what you ate today, according to the rules of Trick 4. Some can go in more than one column - eg ice cream and pizza – you can have some of it OR the whole thing.

pain / fromage / beurre / glace / pizza / viande / jambon / pommes de terre / frites / petits pois / carottes / confiture / pomme / croissant / poire / sauce / soupe / gâteau / hamburger / pâtes / céréales / haricots verts / poisson / tomate / poulet / porc / tomates

J'ai mangé ......

Du (picnic)	De la (red)	Des (plural)	Un / une (whole)

Answers

Du	De la	Des	Un / une
pain	glace	pommes de	glace
fromage	pizza	terre	pizza
beurre	viande	frites	pomme
jambon	confiture	petits pois	croissant
poisson	sauce	carottes	poire
poulet	soupe	pâtes	hamburger
porc		céréales	tomate
chocolat		haricots verts	gâteau
gâteau		tomates	

Testing you on Tricks 1-4

Remember – LIKING is the king of the tricks, and pas de beaucoup de comes second, and we need to check those don't apply before we get to the food rules.

1. I don't like bananas

2. I like tennis

3. I prefer Playstation

4. I love maths but I prefer French

5. I like crisps but I eat chips

6. I like pizza but I'm eating pasta

7. I like playing football

8. I don't have any chocolate

9. I don't have a TV

10. I have lots of friends

11. I don't like watching the TV

12. I don't like eating pizza

13. I don't like pizza

14. I eat pizza

15. I eat a croissant with some jam

16. I like wine a lot

17. I like lots of wines

Answers (brackets show the Trick number that applies)

1. (1) Je n'aime pas les bananes

2. (1) J'aime le tennis

3. (1) Je préfère la Playstation

4. (1) J'adore les maths mais je préfère le français

5. (1,4) J'aime les chips **mais j'ai mangé des frites**

6. (1,4) J'aime la pizza **mais je mange des pâtes**

7. (1) J'aime jouer **au foot**

8. (2) Je n'ai pas de chocolat

9. (2) Je n'ai pas de télévision

10. (2) J'ai beaucoup d'amis / de copains

11. (1) Je n'aime pas regarder la télévision

12. (1) Je n'aime pas manger de la pizza

13. (1) Je n'aime pas la pizza

14. (4) Je mange de la pizza

15. (4) Je mange un croissant avec de la confiture

16. (1) J'aime beaucoup le vin

17. (2) J'aime beaucoup de vins

Trick 5

Present tense e-es-y or so so difficult? This is it!

Remember that sentence and you are half way to present tense heaven. There are three main types of verb in French, ending in –er, -re and –ir

The first column – the er verbs is "easy" (e / es / e **sounds like "easy"**)

Second column – the re verbs is **so so difficult (s s d)**

Third column – the ir verbs is the LAST so th**IS IS IT**

The second half is **ons ez ent** every time, except for the last column where your batteries are running out, you're slowing down and you're adding sleepy snoring sounds to it making **issons issez issent**

Here is a reminder of the pronouns that come before the verbs and what they mean:

Je = "**I**" (but it will be shortened to j' before a vowel)

Tu = "**you**" (singular) – This is used to address one person in the familiar form, so not a shopkeeper or an adult you don't know well. Save it for good friends.

Il = "**he**" (or *it* with masculine objects)

Elle = "**she**" (or *it* – with feminine objects)

On = "**we**" or "**one**" – Most commonly you see it meaning "we", but it is used with impersonal expressions like *on peut* meaning *one can,* or *you can,* and *on doit* meaning *one must,* or *you have to.*

Nous = "**we**" (but you can use "on" instead for "we")

Vous = "**you**" (plural or polite) Use this when addressing a person who is not a good friend yet, or a group of people.

Ils = "**they**" (masculine, or a mixed group of male and female people or things)

Elles = "**they**" (feminine, but if there is one single male or masculine thing or person in there it becomes *ils)*

Below is a chart showing how the three basic types of verb go in the present tense:

Typical -er verb: jouer – to play	Typical -re verb répondre – to answer	Typical -ir verb finir – to finish
je joue tu joues il/elle/on joue nous jouons vous jouez ils/elles jouent	je réponds tu réponds il/elle/on répond nous répondons vous répondez ils/elles répondent	je finis tu finis il/elle/on finit nous finissons vous finissez ils/elles finissent
similar verbs *écouter – to listen* *détester – to hate* *donner – to give* *habiter – to live* *manger – to eat* *parler – to speak* *regarder – to watch* *aimer – to like*	**similar verbs** *vendre – to sell* *descendre – to go down* *entendre – to hear*	**similar verbs** *vomir – to be sick* *choisir – to choose* *ralentir – to slow down* *réagir – to react*

Here are examples of the verbs in action

We play = nous jouons

We finish = nous finissons

She likes = elle aime

You (pl) eat = vous mangez

They hear = ils / elles entendent

You (pl) react = vous réagissez

You (s) go down = vous descendez

They watch = ils / elles regardent

He sells = il vend

I listen = j'écoute

I slow down = je ralentis

We eat = nous mangeons

Now fill in the gaps, checking your answers on the previous page

-ER VERBS	-RE VERBS	-IR VERBS
jouer – to play	**répondre – to answer**	**finir – to finish**
je jou…	je répond…	je fin …
tu jou …	tu répond …	tu fin …
il/elle/on jou …	il/elle/on répond…	il/elle/on fin …
nous jou …	nous répond…	nous fin ………..
vous jou …	vous répond…	vous fin ………..
ils/elles jou…	ils/elles répond…	ils/elles fin………
similar verbs	**similar verbs**	**similar verbs**
*écouter – to ……... *	*vendre – to ……..*	*vomir – to ……...*
habiter – to……...	*descendre – to……...*	*choisir – to ……...*
manger – to ……...	*entendre – to …..*	*ralentir – to……...*
parler – to ……...		*réagir – to ……*
regarder – to ……...		
aimer – to ……...		
détester – to ……		
donner – to …..		

Present tense test

1. We play

2. You (s) go down

3. We choose

4. They watch

5. She likes

6. He sells

7. You (pl) eat

8. I listen

9. We recycle

10. She speaks

11. I like

12. We finish

13. They finish

14. They sell

15. He watches

16. I react

17. They react

18. We eat

19. They live

20. You (pl) choose

More advanced sentences combining tricks 1-5

1. We choose lots of sports

2. They don't eat meat

3. She doesn't eat mushrooms

4. He likes chocolate but they hate chocolate

5. I sell a lot of books

6. They like wine a lot

7. You (s) watch too many horror films (films of horror)

8. The teachers give too much homework

9. I watch fewer films because the teachers give too much homework

Answers to present tense test

1.	We play	nous jouons
2.	You (s) go down	vous descendez
3.	We choose	nous choisissons
4.	They watch	ils / elles regardent
5.	She likes	elle aime
6.	He sells	il vend
7.	You (pl) eat	vous mangez
8.	I listen	j'écoute
9.	We recycle	nous recyclons
10.	She speaks	elle parle
11.	I like	j'aime
12.	We finish	nous finissons
13.	They finish	ils / elles finissent
14.	They sell	ils / elles vendent
15.	He watches	il regarde
16.	I react	je réagis
17.	They react	ils / elles réagissent
18.	We eat	nous mangeons (keep the e on this one)
19.	They live	ils / elles habitent
20.	You (pl) choose	vous choisissez

Answers to advanced sentences

1. We choose lots of sports

   Nous choisissons beaucoup de sports

2. They don't eat meat

   Ils / elles ne mangent pas de viande

3. She doesn't eat mushrooms

   Elle ne mange pas de champignons

4. He likes chocolate but they hate chocolate

   Il aime le chocolat mais ils / elles détestent le chocolat

5. I sell a lot of books

   Je vends beaucoup de livres

6. They like wine a lot

   Ils / elles aiment beaucoup le vin

7. You (s) watch too many horror films

   Vous regardez trop de films d'horreur

8. The teachers give too much homework

   Les profs donnent trop de devoirs

9. I watch fewer films because the teachers give too much homework

   Je regarde moins de films parce que les profs donnent trop de devoirs

TRICK 6   IRREGULAR VERBS – in families

Notice the rhymes – and get used to these pairs and groups of verbs being in families – then when you know one you'll remember the other more easily. The verbs in blue have rhyming friends – so if you know one you will know the other.

	savoir	connaitre	faire	aller
	to know a fact	*to know a person*	*to do*	*to go*
Je	sais	connais	fais	vais
Tu	sais	connais	fais	vas
Il	sait	connait	fait	va
Nous	savons	connaissons	faisons	allons
Vous	savez	connaissez	faites	allez
Ils	savent	connaissent	font	vont

	devoir	boire	recevoir
	to have to	*to drink*	*to receive*
Je	dois *(dwa)*	bois *(bwa)*	reçois *(resswa)*
Tu	dois	bois	reçois
Il	doit	boit	reçoit
Nous	devons	buvons	recevons
Vous	devez	buvez	recevez
Ils	doivent *(dwav)*	boivent *(bwav)*	reçoivent *(resswav)*

	vouloir	pouvoir
	to want	*to be able to*
Je	veux *(verr)*	peux *(purr)*
Tu	veux	peux
Il	veut	peut
Nous	voulons	pouvons
Vous	voulez	pouvez
Ils	veulent *(verl)*	peuvent *(perv)*

Testing Trick 6

1. I can

2. I want

3. I drink

4. I must

5. I go

6. I do

7. He goes

8. We go

9. We can

10. They go

11. We do

12. He does

13. She does

14. He drinks

15. She drinks

16. We drink

17. They must

18. They drink

19. I know (fact)

20. I know (person)

Answers

1. I can   je peux

2. I want   je veux

3. I drink   je bois

4. I must   je dois

5. I go   je vais

6. I do   je fais

7. He goes   il va

8. We go   nous allons

9. We can   nous pouvons

10. They go   ils vont

11. We do   nous faisons

12. He does   il fait

13. She does   elle fait

14. He drinks   il boit

15. She drinks   elle boit

16. We drink   nous buvons

17. They must   ils doivent

21. They drink   ils boivent

22. I know (fact)   je sais

23. I know (person)   je connais

TRICK 7

The past tense is a grey area…. until you see it like this!

The forest of Yesterday

However weird it may sound at first, this trick will help you with the past tense, or *passé composé*. The diagram below shows how this tense has different beginnings which are just different paths into the forest...

*The passé composé begins with **je me suis, je suis** and **j'ai***

The e is acute and the r goes away

You could begin with « le week-end dernier »

This tense uses the é – think of the accent being like a twig on the tree.

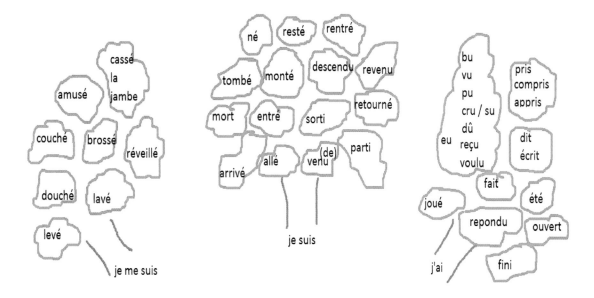

How it works

You start with one of the three beginnings, then use one of the words inside the trees – these are called *past participles*. In English, we might say: I have eaten / fallen, where "eaten" or "fallen" are the past participles.

The **house verbs** belong in the middle section of the forest: JE SUIS allé / (re/de)venu / arrivé / parti / (r)entré / sorti / monté / descendu / tombé / né / resté / retourné

The **bedroom (with an ensuite bathroom) verbs** belong on the left: JE ME SUIS *réveillé / levé / douché / lavé / habillé / brossé les dents / amusé / cassé la jambe / couché*

Every other verb goes on the right, following J'AI (see page 42): J'AI regardé, répondu, fini, pris, compris, appris

Here's a diagram showing the house verbs and bedroom verbs. Try and memorise the picture because you will need to reproduce it on the next page…

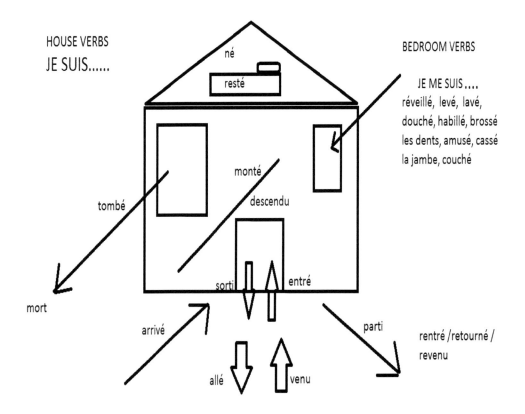

Can you remember where they all go ?

Draw your own house and label it with the past participles of the **je suis** verbs (house verbs) and the **je me suis** verbs, or bedroom verbs.

The J'ai forest

If you are dealing with a verb that is not a bedroom verb or a house verb you can go into the J'ai forest. This part of the forest has a whole variety of trees in it. There are three regular trees because of the general rule for past participles is that:

-er verbs go to é	jouer – to play	j'ai joué – I played
-re verbs go to u	vendre – to sell	j'ai vendu – I sold
-ir verbs go to i	finir – to finish	j'ai fini – I finished

But not all verbs follow this rule. Some take a "u", hence the "U" tree (yew tree). A few will end in "it" and "is" and then a few odd ones sit on their own like "J'ai fait" and "j'ai ouvert".

avoir	--> J'ai eu	I had
boire	--> J'ai bu	I drank
croire	--> J'ai cru	I believed
devoir -	-> J'ai dû	I had to
savoir	--> J'ai su	I knew (fact)
voir	--> J'ai vu	I saw
pouvoir	--> J'ai pu	I was able to
lire	--> J'ai lu	I read
vouloir	--> J'ai voulu	I wanted
recevoir	--> j'ai reçu	I received
vivre	-->J'ai vécu	I lived
prendre -	-> J'ai pris	I took
comprendre	--> J'ai compris	I understood
apprendre	--> J'ai appris	I learnt
mettre	--> J'ai mis	I put
dire	--> J'ai dit	I said
écrire	--> J'ai écrit	I wrote
ouvrir	--> J'ai ouvert	I opened
faire	--> J'ai fait mes devoirs	I did / made
être	--> J'ai été	I was
pleuvoir	--> Il a plu	it rained

This is a memory test like Kim's game. Have another look at the previous page, then on this page see how many of those past participles you can remember and write them down in this box. Eg fait, pris, voulu.....

You have 5 minutes!

Can you draw your own forest now – with a je me suis entrance, a je suis entrance and a j'ai entrance, putting those past participles in the trees with the twigs…

Past tense at the next level

It's not all about me. Or you. In fact, anyone might have done it. So how do you say "*he* finished" or "*they* went" or "*we* returned"?

The answer is simple (ish). Instead of the je form, you are going to need another form of the verb être or avoir, and go from there. Here is a reminder of how they go:

être (to be)	**avoir (to have)**
je suis	j'ai
tu es	tu as
il / elle / on est	il / elle / on a
nous sommes	nous avons
vous êtes	vous avez
ils / elles sont	ils / elles ont

Examples: note that with bedroom and house verbs, the past participle adds an extra e if the person who did it is feminine, and an extra s if they are plural.

Il a fini	He finished
Nous avons ouvert	We opened
Il a pris	He took
Ils sont descendus (extra s!)	They went down
Elles sont montées (extra e and s!)	They went up
Elle est rentrée (extra e!)	She went back
Tu as compris	You understood
Tu es parti	You left

44

Testing you on Trick 7

1. I woke up
2. I got up
3. I went to bed
4. I went
5. I arrived
6. I left
7. I was born
8. I fell
9. I went downstairs
10. I ate
11. I replied
12. I finished
13. I took
14. I said
15. I wrote
16. I did
17. I was able to
18. I had to
19. I saw
20. I drank
21. I broke my leg
22. I received
23. I came home
24. We returned
25. They finished
26. You (s) chose
27. He took
28. She understood

Answers

1. I woke up   je me suis réveillé
2. I got up   je me suis levé
3. I went to bed   je me suis couché
4. I went   je suis allé
5. I arrived   je suis arrivé
6. I left   je suis parti
7. I was born   je suis né
8. I fell   je suis tombé
9. I went downstairs   je suis descendu
10. I ate   j'ai mangé
11. I replied   j'ai répondu
12. I finished   j'ai fini
13. I took   j'ai pris
14. I said   j'ai dit
15. I wrote   j'ai écrit
16. I did   j'ai fait
17. I was able to   j'ai pu
18. I had to   j'ai dû
19. I saw   j'ai vu
20. I drank   j'ai bu
21. I broke my leg   je me suis cassé la jambe
22. I received   j'ai reçu
23. I came home   je suis rentré chez moi
24. We returned   nous sommes retournés
25. They finished   ils ont fini
26. You (s) chose   tu as choisi
27. He took   il a pris
28. She understood   elle a compris

TRICK 8   Zis is Je Vais of ze future

My impression of a German accent has helped students remember that if we're in the future tense, we probably need to start with "je vais".

You know the one – *je vais regarder la télé / je vais aller au cinéma / je vais faire du sport...*

It's just like the English – *I'm going to watch TV / go to the cinema etc.* We use the verb "to go" as well. But don't forget to change the verb *aller* to the right person. Here is a reminder of aller:

Je vais   (zis is je vais of ze future)

tu vas

il va

nous allons (look at the ll and see it as legs, going somewhere!)

vous allez (those legs again)

ils vont

Testing you on Trick 8

1. I'm going to eat

2. He is going to play

3. We are going to go

4. They are going to go out

5. She is going to have to work

6. You (pl) are going to be able to play tennis

7. You (s) are going to come home

Answers

1. I'm going to eat chocolate   je vais manger du chocolat
2. He is going to play tennis   il va jouer au tennis
3. We are going to go to the park   nous allons aller au parc
4. They are going to go out   ils vont sortir
5. She is going to have to work   elle va devoir travailler (2 verbs!)
6. You (pl) are going to be able to play   vous allez pouvoir jouer
7. You (s) are going to go home   tu vas rentrer chez toi

Did you get the last one? *Chez* really means *at or to the house of*. So

Chez moi	at / to my house
Chez toi	at / to your house
Chez lui	at / to his house
Chez elle	at / to her house
Chez nous	at / to our house
Chez vous	at / to your house
Chez eux	at / to their house (boys)
Chez elles	at / to my house (girls)
Chez mon ami	at my friend's house

NB chez has other meanings in more advanced French

TRICK 9   Using aller and the holiday list

To say I go somewhere (present tense, friend of faire) = **je vais**

To say I went (house verb takes je suis) = **je suis allé**

To say I am going to go = **je vais aller**

But what comes next? How do you say where and where you went?

The general rule is:

à + towns   je suis allé à Paris / Disneyland

en + countries   je suis allé en France / Espagne

Stick to European countries and not Portugal or USA to make this rule work – because it's "au Portugal" and "aux Etats-Unis"

With places in the town, the general rule is *"to the"* = *"au",* and this applies when you are going to all the places in the town that sound slightly English, like cinema, park etc. But there is a whole list that take *"à la"* instead:

Imagine a holiday – you go **to the bank** to get money, **to the library** to get some books, to the **bakery and cake shop** to get journey food, then you go **to the station** to get the train. On the holiday you go **to the beach and the pool**, to the **ice rink**, then **to the post office** to send a postcard home.

au (general rule)	à la (holiday list)
parc	banque (bank for the money)
restaurant	bibliothèque (library for the books)
centre sportif	boulangerie (for bread for journey)
collège	patisserie (for the journey cakes)
centre commercial	gare (station to get the train)
cinéma	piscine (pool)
supermarché	plage (beach)
musée	patinoire (ice rink)
magasin	poste (to send a postcard home)

AUX magasins   *A L' école / église (begins with a vowel)*

Fill in the gaps

Le week-end dernier...

Je suis allé .... piscine

Je suis allé .... parc

Je suis allé .... bibliothèque

Je suis allé .... restaurant

Je suis allé .... centre commercial

Je suis allé .... poste

Je suis allé .... plage

Je suis allé .... magasin

Je suis allé .... cinéma

Je suis allé .... collège

Je suis allé .... gare

Je suis allé .... banque

Je suis allé .... café

Je suis allé .... école

Je suis allé .... église

Now check previous page for answers

What about how you got there?

If it's got an **en**gine, it's **en**, which also goes with most countries. So just think that you need an **en**gine to go to another country.

Je suis allé **en France en avion**

en voiture	by car
en car	by coach
en train	by train
en bus	by bus
en bateau	by boat
en tramway	by tram
en camion	by lorry
en hélicoptère	by helicopter
en avion	by plane

But if it hasn't got an engine, use à, which also goes with towns. Just think that you don't need an engine to get to the town – walking or bike will do.

Je suis allé **à Londres à pied**   I walked to London

Je vais aller **à Paris à vélo**   I'm going to cycle to Paris

(the main exception is à moto – but you shouldn't go by motorbike anyway – it's dangerous!)

Can you say where you went on holiday now?

Je suis allé en ………….. en ……………….

And where you went last weekend ?

Je suis allé au / à la …………………………. en / à ……………………..

Before I show you the final trick in the book, let's recap…

1. Liking, hating, preferring
2. Pas de / beaucoup de
3. Jouer for games and fairyland with the activities and beach scene
4. Food and everything else using my red list
5. Present tense easy, so so difficult, this is it
6. Irregular families – learn 9 at a time
7. The forest of yesterday begins with je me suis je suis and j'ai
8. Ziz is je vais of the future
9. Aller and the holiday list

Got it? Ok last one now.

TRICK 10   He makes the weather

Imagine (you don't need to actually believe, just imagine) that God (HE) makes the weather – so that when you say *"il fait beau"* = you think *"he makes beautiful"*.

If you want to say anything about the weather, stick to this rule and talk about il fait or il a fait / il a fait (past tense, *j'ai* forest) followed by *beau, chaud, mauvais* or *froid*. The rest of the weather words you just need to understand for now rather than use.

Il fait beau / mauvais	the weather is good / bad

or in the past

Il a fait beau / mauvais	the weather was good / bad

and in the future

il va faire beau / mauvais	the weather will be good / bad

OTHER WEATHER WORDS

Le soleil brille	the sun is shining
Il y a du brouillard / du vent	It is foggy / windy
Il y avait du brouillard / du vent	It was foggy / windy
il neige	it's snowing
il neigeait	it was snowing
Il a neigé	it snowed
la neige	snow
il pleut	it is raining
il pleuvait	it was raining
il a plu	it rained
il gèle	it is icy
un orage / une tempête	a storm
des nuages	clouds

Now you literally know every trick in the book. You can:

- Say where you normally go, where you went and where you're going to go (using *au / à la*)
- How you go there, went there or are going to go there (using *en / à*)
- What activity you do, did or will do (using *jouer / faire du / faire de la etc*)
- What you eat, ate or will eat (using *un, une, du / de la / des*)
- What the weather is like, was like or will be like (using *il fait*)
- And, more generally, what you like / dislike and why (using *le la les*)

WITHOUT MISTAKES!!!

Testing you on EVERYTHING you have learnt in this book

Translate these paragraphs into French

1. **Present tense**
   Normally I go to the swimming pool by car. I go swimming, eat a burger, some chips and an ice cream. The weather is good. I love swimming because it's fun and easy.

2. **Past tense**
   Last weekend I went to the park on the bus. I played football, ate some crisps and a sandwich. The weather was good. I love playing football because it's great but I prefer rugby.

3. **Future tense**
   Next weekend I'm going to go to the cinema with my friends. I'm going to watch a film and we are going to eat pizza and ice cream. The weather will be good. I don't like romantic films but I love action films because they are exciting.

Answers

1. Normalement je vais à la piscine en voiture. Je fais de la natation, je mange un hamburger, des frites et une glace. Il fait beau. J'adore faire de la natation (OR J'adore la natation) parce que c'est amusant et facile.

2. Le week-end dernier je suis allé au parc en bus. J'ai joué au foot et j'ai mangé des chips et un sandwich. Il a fait beau. J'aime jouer au foot parce que c'est super mais je préfère le rugby.

3. Le week-end prochain je vais aller au cinéma avec mes amis. Je vais regarder un film et nous allons manger de la pizza et de la glace. Il va faire beau. Je n'aime pas les films romantiques mais j'adore les films d'action parce qu'ils sont passionnants.

ESSENTIAL VOCAB LISTS

With memory techniques

CLOTHES (les vêtements)

Imagine the masculine clothes on a boy and the feminine clothes on a girl – you will end up with a very casual looking boy (in trousers, Tshirt, jumper, coat, hat, trainers, gloves and carrying an umbrella) and a smart-looking girl in skirt / dress, shirt, jacket, tie, glasses, shoes and socks…

Masculine clothes

un pull	jumper *(pullover)*
un t-shirt	Tshirt
un pantalon	trousers *(pants that are long)*
un manteau	coat *(for a man, down to his toes)*
un chapeau	hat *(for a chap)*
des gants	gloves *(same g as in English)*
un parapluie	umbrella *(for the pluie = rain)*
un imperméable	raincoat *(impermeable membrane)*
un bonnet	woolly hat
des collants	tights *(colle= glue)*

Feminine clothes

une chemise	shirt
une jupe	skirt
une robe	dress
une veste / un blouson	jacket *(not a vest !)*
des chaussettes	socks *(you need a set of them)*
des chaussures	shoes *(need to be sure of them)*
une cravate	tie *(like a cravat)*
des lunettes	glasses *(little moons – lune=moon)*

une casque	helmet
une casquette	cap *(small helmet)*
des écouteurs	earphones *(listeners, from écouter)*
une écharpe / un foulard	scarf *(in a sharp frost you're a fool not to wear it)*
des bottes	boots
des bijoux	jewellery
du maquillage	make-up
en coton, en laine, en soie, en cuir	made of cotton / wool / silk / leather

BODY (le corps)

le bras	arm *(the first thing that goes into a bra)*
la jambe	leg *(messy breakfast-eater drops jam on leg)*
la tête	head *(the accent is like a little hat on a head)*
la bouche	mouth
les yeux (pronounced "yer")	eyes
les oreilles	ears *(you can hear people shouting "ooray")*
les épaules	shoulders *("hey Paul"- you slap his shoulder)*
les genoux	knees
le nez	nose
les dents	teeth *(think dentist)*
le cou	neck *(cuckoo stretching neck out of the clock)*
le dos (pronounced "doh")	back *(back door sounds like back – dos)*
le ventre / l'estomac	stomach
la main	hand *(the main thing you need to do anything)*

le pied	foot *(think "piedestrian")*
les doigts	fingers
les doigts des pieds	toes *(fingers of feet)*
le cœur	heart *(coronary artery)*
la langue	tongue *(language)*
les joues	cheeks *(go all rosy after playing – jouer)*
J'ai mal à la tete / au bras	my head / arm hurts

TIME (Quand? Quelle heure est-il?)

Il est neuf heures moins le quart	It's 8.45
Il est deux heures et demie	It's 2.30
Il est huit heures et quart	It's 8.15
Il est trois heures vingt	It's 3.20
Il est onze heures moins vingt	It's 10.40
Il est minuit / midi	It's midnight / midday
à + time	at
hier	yesterday ("hiersterday")
demain	tomorrow
dernier	last *(70 denier tights do last!)*
prochain	next *(approaching)*
lundi / mardi …….. dernier / prochain	last / next Monday / Tuesday
la semaine dernière	last week (note the e on both words)
l'année dernière	last year (note the e on both words)
le weekend dernier	last weekend (no e/accent on dernier)
la semaine prochaine	next week (note the e on both words)

60

l'année prochaine	next year (note the e on both words)
le weekend prochain	next weekend (no e on either)
Il y a deux ans	two years ago (there are 2 years between now and then)
Après avoir mangé / ayant mangé	after having eaten
De temps en temps / parfois / quelquefois	sometimes
Tous les jours	every day
Quand j'ai le temps	when I have time
Chaque samedi / tous les samedis / le samedi	every Saturday

FOOD (Je voudrais…   Je prends….   Vous avez…?) THINK PICNIC

du pain	bread
du beurre	butter (bu- - er)
du fromage	cheese
du poulet	chicken
du jambon	ham
du saucisson	sausage (salami style)
du salami	salami
du bœuf	beef
du poisson	fish
du gâteau	cake
du chocolat	chocolate
du sel	salt
du miel	honey
du sucre	sugar

du lait	milk
du vin	wine

USE "de la" IF YOU HAVE A BIT OF IT, AND IT'S FEMININE (red list)

de la viande	meat
de la confiture	jam
de la glace	ice cream
de la pizza	pizza
de la soupe	soup
de la sauce	sauce

USE "de l'" IF THERE IS SOME OF IT AND IT STARTS WITH A VOWEL

de l'agneau	lamb
de l'eau	water *(rhymes with "below" - underground spring…)*

PLURAL FOOD – IF YOU EAT / HAVE LOTS, USE « DES »

des chips	crisps *(not chips!)*
des frites	chips *(fries!)*
des céréales	cereal *(remember it's plural)*
des pâtes	pasta *(remember it's plural pastas)*
des œufs	eggs *(the smell of eggs is – ugh)*
des légumes	vegetables
des pommes de terre	potatoes *(apples of the ground)*
des petits pois	peas *(little peas)*
des haricots verts	green beans

des champignons	mushrooms *(little champions)*
des oignons	onions
des raisins	grapes
des raisins secs	raisins (dry grapes)
des saucisses	sausages
des crêpes	pancakes
des bonbons	sweets
des biscuits	biscuits
des fruits de mer	seafood
des crevettes	prawns
des amis	friends
des gens	people

Un / une – IF YOU EAT / DRINK / OWN THE WHOLE THING
Note – most fruit is feminine, so imagine ladies eating fruit

une poire	pear
une pomme	apple
une banane	banana
une pêche	peach
une orange	orange
une mandarine	satsuma
une mangue	mango
une pastèque	watermelon
une salade	salad

EXCEPT

un ananas	pineapple
un melon	melon

ICE CREAMS AND DRINKS ARE FOR LADIES TOO !

une glace	an ice cream *(de la glace if it's in a bowl)*
une boisson	a drink
une limonade	a lemonade
une bière	a beer

HOT DRINKS FOR BOYS !

un chocolat chaud	a hot chocolate
un café	a coffee
un thé	a tea

GENERAL

un repas	meal
l'addition	bill
le plat du jour	dish of the day
service compris	service included
un pourboire	tip

SCHOOL   (Mon collège)

J'étudie	I study
l'histoire	history
l'informatique	ICT (computing)
l'anglais	English
les maths	maths
les sciences	science
le sport	sport
le latin	Latin
le dessin	art
le français	French
la géographie	geography
la musique	music
l'EPS	PE
Ma matière préférée c'est	My favourite subject is
J'ai neuf cours par jour	I have 9 lessons a day
Chaque cours dure	Each lesson lasts
la récréation	break time
la pause déjeuner	lunch break
Les profs nous donnent trop de devoirs	The teachers give us too much homework
Je suis forte en	I'm good at
Je suis nulle en	I'm bad at
J'ai de bonnes notes	I get good marks
J'ai de mauvaises notes	I get bad marks

TOP TIP

Ma matière préférée – it's your favourite – so 3 cheers – 3 UP accents

préfère – you prefer it, you're not that sure, the accents look like sad eyebrows

JOBS – les métiers *(this is the only time you don't need a little word before the noun – je suis prof NOT je suis un prof)*

un facteur	a postman *(a factory of letters)*
un vendeur	a sales assistant *(a vending machine sells things)*
un professeur	a teacher
un chauffeur	a driver
un médecin	a doctor
un pharmacien	a chemist *(pharmacist)*
un chirurgien	a surgeon *(sounds like shurgeon)*
un comptable	a accountant *(compter = to count)*
un avocat	a lawyer *(lawyers are advocates)*
un informaticien	an IT consultant
un ingénieur	an engineer
un pompier	a fireman *(think pumps)*
un gendarme	a policeman *(a gentleman who may be armed)*
une infirmière	a nurse *(from the infirmary)*

JOBS around the house

Je passe l'aspirateur	I vacuum *(respiration, breathes in dirt)*
Je fais la vaisselle	I wash up *(vessels are containers)*
Je lave la voiture	I wash the car *(lather sounds like lave)*

Je fais du jardinage	I do the gardening
Je range ma chambre	I tidy my room (arrange my chamber)
Je mets la table	I lay the table (meh)
Je sors les poubelles	I take the rubbish out

Leisure activities

JOUER = TO PLAY (games and instruments)

jouer au foot, rugby, cricket, hockey, tennis, golf, netball, basket, volley

jouer aux échecs	to play chess
jouer aux cartes	to play cards
jouer du piano	to play piano
jouer de la guitare	to play guitar
jouer à l'ordinateur	to play computer
jouer sur la Xbox	to play on the Xbox
jouer sur la Playstation	to play on the Playstation

FAIRE = TO DO (activities which are not games –no balls in Fairyland)

faire du sport	do sport (you don't play sport, you do it)
faire du patinage	go skating (pat the ice to see if it's hard)
faire du vélo / cyclisme	go cycling
faire du VTT	go mountain biking
faire du judo / karaté	do judo, karate
faire de la natation	go swimming
faire de la voile	go sailing (turn the v upside down for the sail)
faire de la planche a voile	go windsurfing (plank with sail)

faire de la plongée	go diving (plunge)
faire de la gymnastique	do gym
faire de la danse	dance
faire de l'équitation	go horseriding
faire de l'athlétisme	do athletics
faire de l'escrime	do fencing (scream !)
faire de l'escalade	go climbing (escalator)
faire de l'alpinisme	go mountaineering (in the Alps)
faire des promenades / randonnées	go on walks / hikes

At home (Mum owns the house, car, road, the whole town…)

Notice that all the rooms in the house, and a lot of the things around the house are feminine (house, door, window, car, shelves, wardrobe, TV). Imagine that the only place Dad is allowed is office and sitting room – and garden. He can also have a bed, a computer, a pen and a few other bits (see second list below) but he has to do the housework (le ménage)

une maison individuelle	a detached house
une maison jumelée / mitoyenne	a semi-detached / terraced house
une cuisine	a kitchen
une salle à manger	a dining room
une salle de bains	a bathroom
une chambre	a bedroom (like a chamber)
une véranda	a conservatory
une armoire	a wardrobe (you keep your armour in it)
une étagère	a bookshelf (has étages like floors)
une voiture	a car
une table	a table

une chaise	a chair
une porte	a door
une fenêtre	a window
une moquette	a fitted carpet
une lampe	a lamp
une commode	a chest of drawers
une piscine	a swimming pool
une machine à laver	a washing machine
une cuisinière	a cooker
une télévision	a TV
une Xbox	an Xbox
une ville	a town
une rue	a road

Picture Dad in these rooms only

un salon	a sitting room (like a hairdressing salon)
un jardin	a garden
un grenier	an attic
un bureau	an office

He can sit on

un canapé	a sofa
un fauteuil	an armchair
un lit	a bed

for entertainment he can have un livre (a book) and un ordinateur (a computer) **and his job is** le ménage (housework)

Grave accent words

There aren't too many of these in words that are commonly used, but don't lose marks unnecessarily by forgetting the ones you should know.

après	after
très	very
près de	near
mère / père / frère / grand-mère / grand-père	mother, father, brother etc
première (with fem noun)	first
deuxième, troisième etc	second, third etc
derrière	last
derrière	behind
lumière	light
à (eg à gauche / à londres)	on the left / to london
où	where (without accent = *or*)
là	there (without accent = *the*)
je me lève	i get up
j'espère	i hope
j'achète	i buy
je préfère (sad eyebrow accents !)	i prefer
problème	problem
déjà	already
élève	pupil
collège	school
bibliothèque	library
matière	subject
complètement	completely
mystère	mystery

Here's a story to help you remember the grave accent words :

Where do I live? I live **there**, in a **very** big house **near** London **behind** the **library**, with my **mother, father, brother, grandmother** and **grandfather.** I **hope I get up** and **buy** something - but the **problem** is that I **already** have to go to **school** and be a **pupil** studying a **subject** and I **prefer** the days where it's **completely** a **mystery**

Using that story, see how many grave accent words you can remember and write them below:

Very French things

un Parisien	person from Paris
le TGV	train grande vitesse (fast train)
le SNCF	French railway company
le VTT	mountain biking
les randonnées	hiking
la chasse	hunting
la boulangerie	bakery
la pâtisserie	cake shop
quinze jours	a fortnight
le lycée	sixth form college
un département	similar to a county of france
les escargots	snails

False friends

la location DOESN'T MEAN LOCATION	rental
la librairie DOESN'T MEAN LIBRARY	bookshop
personne DOESN'T always MEAN PERSON	nobody
passer les examens DOESN'T MEAN PASS EXAMS	take exams
un roman DOESN'T MEAN ROMAN	novel
la journée DOESN'T MEAN JOURNEY	day
assister DOESN'T MEAN ASSIST	attend
actuellement DOESN'T MEAN ACTUALLY	now
attendre DOESN'T MEAN ATTEND	wait FOR
raisins DOESN'T MEAN RAISINS	grapes

The words everyone forgets

sans	without
presque	almost
devant	in front of
souvent	often
avant	before
derrière	behind
près de	near
loin de	far from
depuis	since (use with present tense!)
il y a	ago (with time) or there is
pour	to (with infinitive) or for (with noun)
puisque	(like parce que) - because
qui	who
quand	when
combien de	how many
trop de	too many (with noun – trop de pollution)
trop	too (with adj – c'est trop difficile)
assez de	enough (with noun – assez de sucre)
assez	quite (with adj – je suis assez grande)
surtout	especially, above all
malheureusement	unfortunately
toujours	always (same number of syllables as the english)
tous les jours	every day (same number of syllables as the english)
déjà	already

Thank you for purchasing this book. I hope it has been helpful.

If so, I would be very grateful if you would give the book a review on Amazon.

If you have any questions please do contact me through my website
www.lucymartintuition.co.uk

You may also be interested in my other books, also available on Amazon:

How to Ace your French Oral

How to Ace your Spanish Oral

How to Ace your German Oral

French vocabulary for GCSE

Spanish vocabulary for GCSE

Common Entrance French Handbook

Brush up your French

NOTES

30137257R00044

Printed in Great Britain
by Amazon